melt

Sarah Hymas

First published in 2020
by Waterloo Press (Hove)
95 Wick Hall
Furze Hill
Hove BN3 1NG
Printed in Palatino 10pt by
One Digital
54 Hollingdean Road
East Sussex BN2 4AA

Cover image: © Winter Sea III © Estate of Joan Eardley. All
Rights Reserved, DACS 2020. Image courtesy the Fleming
Collection.

Author photograph © Floris Tomasini

A CIP record for this book is available from the British Library

ISBN: 978-1-906742-63-8

Acknowledgements

Quote from 'Sea Change' by Jorie Graham in *Sea Change* (Carcanet Press, 2008) by kind permission of Carcanet Press. Quote from 'I am My Home' by Maya Chowdhry in *Fossil* (Peepal Tree Press, 2018) by kind permission of the author.

'This wall' was shortlisted in the 2019 Hinterland nonfiction prize. A version of 'Moist' first appeared in *Not a Drop* (Beautiful Dragons, 2016). 'Whale-boned Corset and Other Relics' was featured in *And Other Poems*, 2018, and highly commended for the Forward Single Poem Prize 2019. 'Recovery' was part of a sequence that was shortlisted for the Ivan Juritz Prize for Creative Experiment in 2017. It features in the artistbook of the same name, held in the National Poetry Library, London.

Some of the text for 'Lido' comes from www.undark.org/article/high-seas-conservation-exploration. 'Towards a Stranding' also exists as a soundscape featuring Steve Lewis on shruti and guitar, and can be heard at www.sarahhymas.net/towards-a-stranding. 'Sea of Whiteness, as Glacier' riffs off Sara Ahmed's 'Phenomenology of Whiteness' (*Feminist Theory*, vol. 8.2, 2007).

Many thanks to editors of *Antiphon*, *The Clearing*, *The Compass*, *Lune*, *Lighthouse Journal*, *Modernist Review*, *Smoke* and *Tenebrae*, who published versions of these poems.

The 'melt' sequence came about after my participation in the Arctic Circle Residency in June 2018, and grew from correspondences with Andrea Krupp, Rachel Honnery, Sarah McCarry, Caroline Pick and Vanessa Vaughan, and conversations with Bulent Diken and Floris Tomasini. Many thanks to the AHRC for funding that trip.

Many many thanks to my writing community for keeping me and the poems buoyant throughout, especially to Maya Chowdhry, Naomi Foyle, Deryn Rees-Jones, Ruby Robinson, Marli Roode, Pauline Rowe, Jill Rudd and Helen Tookey.

And lastly, not leastly, my enduring gratitude for encountering *Sunshine*, and all who skippered and sailed her, for the joy of learning how to be at sea.

List of illustrations

Consider
the body of the ocean which rises every instant into
me

Jorie Graham

Sometimes I fall in love   descend
        from the pinnacle, swim out of the open door.

Maya Chowdhry

The point of vanishing stability

A mast swings through ninety degrees, tipping
and straightening, reined by wind.
Buoyancy: ingrained belief.

The channel a broken glass we kick
into phlegmatic sunshine.
This fire—oil-slicked surface
spread by wind—earth memory burning: coal older than wood.

The story of a grandmother's death retold
until skin unbattens. Imperative lives in the chest.

A worm erupting mud,
oxygenating sands
visible by shadows thrown on flat wet.
Some will fossilise. Some won't.

PCBs swill in trenches, in copepods
eaten by what we will eat.

A fisherwoman up to her waist in water, fighting
to net the fish as they fight to be free:
fishmuscle wrestling armmuscle.
Cutting one open she finds a whole guillemot
dead-nesting in its stomach,
feathers still glossy black.

Crab outgrows its shell, casts it off
softbodied
until the new one grows.

Another tilt will reveal
more fossils at the edge of a desert.
We swing through ninety degrees: jet stream,
earth sliding, ice melt.

[3]

This Wall
Path

Between the lighthouse keeper's cottage and the remains of the abbey a narrow path courses the seawall. It traces where the dyked field drops as wall, part grass, part stone, to beach. You walk it in wind, rain, sunshine, all three simultaneously, or an eerie vacuum. You exchange greetings with other walkers, pass in silence or pass no one. You walk at high tide, low tide, between tides, collecting driftwood, unidentifiable plastic, kindling. Each you treat as a token you carry back to the keeper's cottage, which is your home now, where it is transformed into fuel, tool or relic.

You joke that when you met the man you moved here for you didn't know if you fell in love with him or where he lived. It isn't a joke, of course. It's a hedging of bets as to how you might inhabit this place, how it inhabits you.

To in-habit: to be clothed by a place—wear it—as a monk might his robes—as a sponge might the water around it; or to in-habit: as routine, being informed by the place in which you and others act. You appreciate the intellectual ease of decimal metrics but love how the imperial system truly measures your body's traversing of world: your thumb an inch; a foot the length of a foot; a stride a yard. You pace the wall's length, five hundred paces, half a mile, dividing land from water.

Another Place

I forget what was said. An argument. Discussion. Exchange perhaps.
                                                            How
to turn it over with me rolling inside, rattling, a cog but flesh.

Perhaps in the photo I will notice something more.

    I stack the shell I brought back on top of another shell,
and thumb them into an articulated pyramid in my pocket.
                                To stare at the screen:
is to summon heat exhaustion, drinking shade;

is to rifle through data, hoarded as exabytes on shelves over shelves
                        in a warehouse. Sweden. Ireland.
I try to understand how the servers work: cold weather storage.
It is cold enough here sometimes. But not enough space.

                        Each shell is filled
by the shell inside, not quite fitting.

Sometimes even the depths of my body feel too distant.

Slipway

A power station, battery-squat on the estuary's other shore, will be decommissioned anytime after fifteen years. Meanwhile it continues to pump out three million litres of seawater, used for the cooling system, every minute, warming the immediate waters by ten degrees, fostering larger than average fish. The story goes that constructors threw their hard hats into the setting concrete to ensure the station's walls would withstand even a plane flying into them.

It stands opposite the first slipway that curves from the path down to the beach. By the second it's behind you, forgotten in the view across the bay and beyond, to where tides flow into the Irish Sea. Only one of the slipways is still used by fishermen and wildfowlers to access the beach, by 4x4s now rather than the whammels built to accommodate the shallow bay. At low water mud, shingle and rocks lie exposed at the base of the nearest slip. Sometimes you descend it and follow the track to the Victorian lighthouse at the estuary mouth. Its first and last keepers were women, Janet and Beatrice, whose menfolk fished the bay, repaired boats, worked at the dock. The women would fetch oil and new wicks for the light, polish its mirrors and repair the glass, walking back and forth over the rocky shore at low tides. Now automated, the beacon still marks the mouth of the estuary and guides ships to the nearby dock. And while you can't see its flash since the repair, its tall white structure, bronze cupola and windvane is clearly visible from the cottage's one seaward window. The cottage was built at a time when sea was to be hunkered away from, rather than viewed through double-glazed patio doors.

Wild Swan
after Hans Andersen

The story does not end
with the marriage of the beautiful people.
I believe the brother with a wing for an arm
is the hero. The weight of it buckles his knees, betrays
his heart, snarled as the nettle shawl that failed him,
splicing avian with human blood.

Ankled to saltmarsh, he'll watch swans fly
his wingarm grubby and itching
though unstung by his sister's intentions,
unless this is what she designed.
It was he who laid his head on her lap
whose wings she stroked.

Already she understands entanglement. Love
is blind and can be silent, the story tells us.
Love disrupts.

As the birds beat north, he'll feel the lure
of something he cannot name, something
scarring the fascia seizing his heart in place,
something that charms his neck long, shoulders back
to counterbalance the bulk of his stomach,
that makes his feet redundant, except they're not.
He needs them fixed as he is, as he needs walls and roof
on the saltmarsh, and the window he waits by

with the load of this distant family on his back.
On their return, the glass obscures the keen air
and smell quilting them from him.

Still his sister (because he is her brother
and although he may curse her stupidity
she finds unremitting patience) will bring
wet kelp and scurvy grass, sit with him and ask,
as I might ask you: How is it? What ought I to know?

Concrete

You pass through a stiff kissing gate without affecting its angle, as if a wisp of nothing much at all. You walk invisibly, white, middle-aged, adding your incremental freight to the wall. A ragged slap of concrete funnels into the unsealed path, keeping grass down. Despite its appearance of freshness it is endemic: most concrete is bound by sand mined from the seabed. Splodges plug the seawall against spates of sea and wind. A coarser mix extends along the wall's footing in parts, a wonky seam that barely delineates wall from beach.

Less than an hour away, a deflated balloon, creased and muddy, will plaster a boulder at the slipway base. You'll uncrease it and bin it. From there it'll end up as landfill and leach into the water table; still, less ferocious than choking a fish, seal or jelly.

Grit-eyed

I always think of the beach as free. I did not pay to enter.
            My exchange here is something else.
Collecting plastic makes me part of a place.
Apart from the me who works to earn
the time to be here. Today, though, there is no plastic—
            it has been blown away, under, to shreds.

                              *

However wrapped I am, this scattering
    will chafe a blossoming.
            Turbines overpowered by wind, immobile.
                Screw the wind.   Unscrewed by it.

                              *

I seek out the black shells, their twisted shine. I prefer the stones
hosting barnacles. I saw a pineapple—a whole pineapple—and
                                    did not take it. Fumble
with words. I do not want to talk—I am at the beach. I want to ask
                questions   I cannot answer.

                              *

There must be drawers full of batteries: jumbled rechargeables,
single-use, never quite throwawayable. Friction works
magic to conjure another few minutes—hours—from those
            considered dead.
Years later an Ever Ready Blue washes up
                        fizzing a remote / close hazard
            on my tongue.

                              *

Tideline mosaic:
every upright: crane, turbine, ship, body: holds a slither of stillness
                        behind it. I
am unsure what I hold. Electric skin. Invites a spilling.
        I am not interested in the human
                        rather the sea-ness of me.

Sand

At the second slipway, a suggestion of holiday-brochure beach accumulates at the wall's foot. Possibly once wall, possibly fresh sand, it's colonised by two sandcastles with moats and shell embattlements. Handprints pattern their walls and impressions of knees pock the ground around them. While elsewhere sand mined for beachfront hotels will take years to slide back into the sea, these miniature castles will last a week of neap tides before flattening under springs. They'll be trampled by birds, your own unintentional scuffing, if the water is calm and you're down there to get closer to its long flat sheen. Apart from the lighthouse you are the tallest thing on the beach. A second sentinel.

Sandstone furnishes the majority of the seawall in pink blocks, originally part of the abbey that stood in the fields until the Reformation. Before the abbey the land hosted a leper colony, garrisoned by the saltmarsh. Larger yellow sandstone, lining the lower portion of wall, once lay as great submerged slabs. According to Bob, son of Beatrice, the light's last keeper, the yellow stone becomes less resilient when it's exposed to air. Any erosion is barely evident but for a superficial pitting. At 300 million years old, it has prevailed over the Maersk container that washed up to be sucked into the channel sands over a compelling fortnight, and will long outlast the next.

Moist

In the unfathomable dark
of my closed eyes
microscopic life surfaces
to feed on digested sunlight
or suspended specks: synthetics
that will plug guts and cling
to filaments and furca
of these translucent drifters
some as long as whales
whose gels and gases
upwell smaller than the sleep
I wipe from my lashes.

Stone

The pink abbey stones can be held in two hands, cupped as if receiving or making a blessing. Gleaned from the razed building, they were packed with shale and pebbles before concrete. Keeping sea in its place must have been back-breaking, hernia-inducing work. You enjoy the thought of a transplanted seabed, just as you do when walking inland alongside dry-stone walls. You see in those walls galaxies of compressed calcite shells shed by plankton that have slowly risen through submerged miles of hillside, erupted as limestone to be broken down into enclosures across the county.

The yellow stone was also used for the cottage walls. Janet and her family outgrew the four clapboarded-rooms of the original, landbound light, and extended their home. They had to crook the cottage to avoid the road and continue for another room's length. Right on the road verge, the cottage trembles when the milk lorry rounds the corner to the farm but has, so far, withstood waves, tree trunks and other brash thrown in storm surges. From the upstairs window you've watched tides surf over the embankment and flood past the cottage footings, thrilled by the charge outside, assuming you'll only be housebound until the sea recedes.

Whale-boned Corset and Other Relics

How I loved the net flaring around my thighs,
blue smocking smoky organza
into fingertip deep slots
of mussel black nibbling my chest.
The power of an unscrutinised body.
I *was* the dress. And so, the loch
biting my arms as I exalt
its sting of marbled August, cutting
my fingers as they pull through
resisting cold—remote luxury
for the nicked and wrapped palms
of those girls gutting and rousing herring.
Scales tip between us—between profit and
water—between herring and cod, ploughed
with gunmetal and the slippery tongue
of empire: big fish eating little fish
eating our own cellular change.
Even the black gridlines of salmon cages
moored further up the loch
will away, on the fluke of cheap nature.
To pull on this is to feel already a memory
a fraying seam of two seas colliding.

Holes

The seawall remains under the remit of the Environmental Agency, although for how much longer is a case for budget allocation and arguments of population density. You regard your walking as a form of monitoring. The suddenness of collapse has its genesis in all the fractures and crannies that, if you consider at all, you see as apertures for new plants. After a storm two men come to check for holes, assess repair costs, appraising movement in one direction only. Nitrogen, potassium, chalk and other fertilisers seep from fields into the bay, where the swift tides take them out to sea. At low water a network of rills in the estuary banks reveals the circuitry of the passing of land to sea.

At your bend in the river the saltmarsh is wide, a maze of creeks filling and draining their oily water on the tides. Downriver, at the estuary mouth, the shoreline is shorn to thin-necked clods. You're told the marsh is carried, every seven years, from one side of the bay to the other, and wonder how long this regularity will continue.

Tourist

What is encoded   is felt
in a nubbing of synapses   forcing a rerun:

a man claiming octopus   have more ways of expressing
than things   they need to communicate

: that webby spasm of underwater   flesh
speaking as   only muscle can: lipping

another language to draw myself   closer: *pulpo*
stewing in purple: limbs   ghosting semaphore

from hot copper vats   by benches, plated trestles:
    woodsmoke smudging their circling suction:

pulpo   I mouth again: attach myself: that day now
reduced to a tapas of metal water flesh: an invitation

from another who is not Hokusai   who explains
how he would finger : I   listen : I want to apologise:

oh, *pulpo,* I know   simmering, limbless: detached
at a fiesta where I pivot ignored: un   known

as the nurse   who says be calm
and I am becalmed: in irons   : my sails slack

as if I can be   eight and fortyeight: stopped
in speechlessness, *pulpo*: prop   elled

by not possessing   what I need to say:
brain signing   across all those years between us:

Moss

Moss as marsh, as fixative, as filter, punctuates the wall as lime-brown bobbles that plug as the cement is dislodged. Walking over it demands attention as to how each foot is placed on this unmade remade terrain. Your ankles twist easily, like pebbles grinding as they bear you. No matter how much you repeat the walk down the slope or across the rocks at the wall's foot it never becomes effortless. You have to breathe slowly, holding the moment when inhale turns to exhale, or exhale to inhale, the point of aspiration.

When your neighbour Ralph, who'd lived here for ninety-three years, left for a short stay in a nursing home, bright-eyed and shiny-faced like a newborn, he said he wouldn't be coming back. He didn't, but nor has he left, not for you. Your knowledge of the estuarine field names—Dead Man's Butts, Greasy Pike, Piper Hill—comes from him. He isn't your only filter of the place. It accumulates gradually within you, only just slower than the internet out here streams its information. Despite never seeing it, you know where the cottage's well was, and its miracle sink pumping briny water into the house, because of Bob. It's your partner who clocks the arrival of pink-foot geese, the golden plover roost, flocking godwits. Gav, chimney sweep and purveyor of eels, keeps you abreast of fish numbers, depending on what's in his net. You gather their knowledge, treating it as substantial as all the other keepsakes brought in on the sea.

Driftwood

We could be pall-bearers
slouching home with a spine of dead elm shoulder high.

         Our pacing co-ordinated
   to preserve length, coupling

  limbs gnarled arms
caught around the knot of memory
              we listen
     to the squeal of salt-logged sinew
skinned in the North Atlantic Drift.

Rain makes everything slippery.

Trunk straight: trunk crooked: trunk compressing trunks
where we were so buoyant:
there's no rolling free from the Gulf Stream's fate.

We reel on, awkward
        on uneven ground
    with the weight of a warm nest.

Judder as we heat: forward curl
under this unwieldy pressure, buffeted by wind.
    I eye the grain
  of our lineage, brine pulped.

      We are not myth, ancient or rotting,
not yesterday, but today and tomorrow.
Our niche as scavengers
   we convey this rootless tree
     as others carry unborn children.

Wrack

For centuries the cottage garden has benefitted from seaweed. The soil is rich and crumbly. A sprawl of bladderwrack often collects on the southern edge of the wall footing, within easy reach of the slipway. You fork clumps of it into your wheelbarrow, and relish its springiness, become agile with its lightness. Home-grown vegetables supplemented plover and curlew, as well as flatties and salmon from the river for all the lighthouse keepers. Barrowing the wrack to the cottage you shadow not only them but the monks and, further back, the Neolithic gatherers. It may be why the plot is higher than the encompassing land. You wheel the weed purposefully, savouring each bouncing step.

Long after the tide withdraws, shallow biomes cupped in the wall's footing thrive with barnacles, limpets, whelks grazing on microscopic algae enriched by nitrogen phosphorus run-off. Beyond the rocks, lugworm casts butte the mudflats, and beyond that a glacial canyon plunges out to sea. No hint of it in the corrugated seaskin or drying mud. Perhaps forty times deeper in parts than the wall is high, it is a close, silted place of chemicals and heat. Salmon, arriving from Iceland to spawn, must sense it from miles offshore. They've declined by hundreds compared to two years ago. Next year even fewer will breed, so fewer again will return.

Recovery

However much your body disturbs you
it needs to be loved

like this beach
you mine for bottles

filled with sour congealment,
screwed grit and fish scales.

Where fork prongs and splintered cups
strewn across grass and shells

are called confetti
which you collect and bin

because in the deep
nothing breaks down to nothing.

Skear

The wall bends back inland to edge another, smaller river running to join the estuary. Between them, before they merge, a low promontory banks off the wall, providing the easiest place to drop down onto the beach. You call this finger of land the skear, a word-remnant of the Norse skjær and Scottish skerry. It curves round to where the channel light stands. This light was the lower of two. The upper light is gone but for a concrete imprint in your garden. The two lights had to be aligned by ships entering the estuary for the dock. A year or so back a tanker ran into the remaining light. During its repair each block was laid out on the skear for months. Blocks, half a metre long, a quarter thick, were numbered, all slightly curved, bedded down into the shale and shells. You would walk among the disassembled pillar, pick a stone to lie back on, legs swinging against its side. It was so much more imposing and intimate in this new formation.

Unlike a footprint on the moon, deep as the day it was made, the tracks between the slipway, blocks and where they now rise again as tower, are being sluiced flatter by tides. There's no trace of where it was once dispersed. The bellying skear is fed shale and shingle by the two rivers. The lower light, with its fresh white paint, is solid as ever, beaming out every night. It's reflected in the light that stands on the north side of the bay, whose flash, once every fifteen seconds, you can see from your window. In daylight you stare north but can only guess where exactly it is. After dark, with the red lights of the windfarm, things become temporarily more fixed. Renting the cottage ensures you shallow-roots; that your landlady's family has lived around here for centuries drills your rhizomes deeper. You attempt a smooth growth between the two.

Intertide

A rock ladles the thought of a body reclining
            among protruding bedrock migrating to grit.

Lines of Flight

I am trying to savour pegging each garment to the line
rather than pinch this task of my mother, her mother
and hers.

Gusts of thirty-five miles an hour slap
prehensile legs and arms—me wet and cold.

Someone is berating:
You have not acquired a maternal patience.

Another net pins an octopus wide,
ringed suckers proud along its splayed marble body.

When I catch my heart push against
the swimmy blue flesh of an inside wrist—

I wonder what stops us feeling
the flush of blood through our body.

You ought to consider yourself lucky
living in a place where clothes can dry outside year-round.

Not all are mine.   This trajectory of remote selves
yanking at the cord between house and sea wall.
Just their impetus.

The octopus is taut—its tentacled brain shock-wired
as we try to disentangle blanched tips clasping the strings.

In Finland friends bring in midwinter boards
of sheets and towels, drunk dry by continental air. Yes
we have compared washing stories.

Here, the fabric's damp
will reach the plants eventually. The detergent too.

It is not my hand bending back waxy digits
                        attempting an unwrinkling of tense.

Light shines through the weave thinning with every wash
        its artillery of microfibres split and charging.

The flapping clothes insist all is well:
                a breezy faith they'll be worn again.

Lurching forward—knotted—we leer over the trapped creature
    urging it off. Out. Away. I am tied. Not simply by gravity.
        Whatever it is—is stubborn.

                Until flipping. Plunged red.
                                Flushed scarlet
it pulses through water. Brighter
                for the white it was less than a second ago.

Sleek now. Bullet riding zippered straits.
                A bloody gleam beating in the swill.

Boulder

Talk is of the channel being left to silt up, the dock decommissioned
in favour of a larger port near the power station. Yet this brings no
sense of land security. Across the estuary the sandy spit of the point
has no legislative protection, only boulders paid for by another
family whose local ancestry goes back generations. Its community
paid for sea defences to be built around the 19th century grave of a
young African man, memorialised as 'Samboo'. His status, like his
name, is disputed: slave, servant or freeman, depending on who's
talking. He died, variously, of heartbreak for his master, pneumonia,
or smallpox. History is contingent on tongues as the sand of the
point is on the sea's suck beneath the boulders.

The same imported boulders bolster parts of the wall you treat as
solid ground, tamping it with each sure step. What looks like a large
iceberg is caught between them. Two of you will have to come back
to carry it. Then you'll discover it's polystyrene. Later still you learn
it's part of a pontoon from a marina hundreds of miles away,
smashed by a storm weeks earlier. You haul it more awkwardly than
you anticipated. Beads fly off, catch in your throat, stopper breath.

Lido

Fattest primate I breaststroke under
                      onshore squalling: head to wind: ten times
as many fat cells as any other animal my size:
                      mandating protection: knuckles beyond blue:
arms on automatic: a legally binding instrument:
                      two hundred nautical miles from shore is beyond
all national jurisdiction. Fish caught on high seas
                      bring in $16 billion annually. Benefits of protection
outweigh the cost. Humans accumulate fat
                      before birth: elbows bend, straighten.
This last weekend before winter I swim
                      through bullet points: rain. A gull guides me,
my head dipping in and out of water unlike
                      other land mammals. Phytoplankton incorporate
atmospheric carbon dioxide into biomass: back and forth.
                      Cold spears glutes. Seizes shoulders. Fat for buoyancy.
Algae provide $148 billion per year of social benefit
                      from curtailed warming. Some fat is white fat.
This tiled circle is a no-take reserve.
                      Body more purple than white.
Penguin is also a perpendicular creature. I continue:
                      conscious control: withstand more hammering
of a cost-benefit analysis: how
                      my descended larynx enables me to investigate
0.01% of the seafloor in detail: spleen: gulping:
                      ecological triage: prescription for depression:
one more crossing: cyan below,
                      grey above. I weep alongside the walrus and sea otter:
Omega-3 abundant in seagrass: feeds my brain tissue:
                      back and forth:

Bioluminescence

      Hurling water overboard we ignite
this creased evening.
                    Adrenaline
sparks my arm, my chest
      as if I'm watching my thrill
            glitter
          in nebula exploding below.

        A circuitry faster than I can distinguish
anything from myself, itself or ourselves
flashes in the shadow of the hull
         flaking antifoul   coppering
              barnacles and algae
        for the length of our voyage
ensuring some speed but nothing compared to this.

There is no cellular speed compared to this
        hundred millisecond bluewhite charge
      carried through water.

                    Water that sings
through blood and brain, perhaps causing a different
stress, deep in unconsidered cells, flashing
and sparking their alarm.
        Pin bright to deter predators.

Not us. We throw again. Again!
Without knowing whether what we deplete
                will be recharged,
or if these are the same few creatures responding over and over—

which they can't be when you think of how their blooms
of nightblue or dayred surface-smears
                              curve with currents, turn colossal
                    continental, when viewed from a satellite:

visible only by detachment:

           just as my silhouette swims solo
                              beneath the sun beneath me:
                    shot through by minnows
             eel-inking each rock and sponge.

        The sea lifts me
                    away from me
                              surrendering me to my mechanics:
separate and contingent

                    on the constellation spraying
                         through droplets   this small arc
             of an arm swinging through one summer night.

Cracks

Higher crevices in the wall will, in early summer, sprout thrift and campion, obscuring mussel shells whose beds have not been farmed due to mercury contamination. Increased acid in seawater weakens the byssus attaching them to rock, making it easier for birds to tug them free.

As many turbines as empty shells stitch the bay, most spinning in the sunlight but some broken out of sync. They split the wind into hundreds of streams, but from this distance you feel it in a singular force, buffeting you landwards. Hundreds more will be erected, stapling a fence the water will continue to flow through. The incoming current closes the gap between you and them so there is no space between you, just as the parts of this wall are held together, and you to it, by whatever renders you to your own ambiguous fortifications.

Slow Rising

One lobster in a wreckage
of brittle stars, urchins, clam husks, crabs, lugworm casings—
possibly millions of splayed limbs desiccated in the stretch of miles
        that will become beach. And we
              may not save its life—merely prolong
                     (agony, how to know
if squeal is emotion or escaping air)
another hour—tide.

                  Perhaps we want
to save ourselves.   We know
we cannot revive the dead—reverse days—rehydraulicise
hearts with photographs of toddlers
and terriers playing in the dunes.

(It is the act of picking it up
of passing it between us and dropping it and
blaming the other and trying
to ascertain if it is the wind or it
teasing its tentacles
then carrying it towards the sea and into a pool
where its mandibles twitch a bubble
and legs blush a slow rise indigo
at the same rate of our own thawing
that stays the pain.)

        Stalling
our rising defences.   Those once mottled legs creeping
blue with lobster life
  —these few seconds we bend over
               the beads of air—
      ourselves a slow blush of resistance to the immobility
             of wrack darkening—we don't know
if it will live—but our bodies know love
as an act of resistance.

Runes

These bits of wrack are not things as much tools:
rope that could haul you out of water.

Notes to a song I must know.
To study them, as myself without a name,

brings our bodies back
to what has made us, what will make us.

I have tasted the salt bitterness of union
and want more.

Tongues licking an unfamiliar language
soften any jackhammer into a music

I can dance with
and twist against the violence of light.

I do not believe the lithium battery
of the moon is so far away.

The future is already here
in what these wild findings divine.

*

My hands are birthing hands
warm, wet enough to incubate eggs

stolen unwittingly from the shingle
with everything else we brought back

for tonight's reading. I was as indiscriminate
as the future that is your future is my future.

I didn't expect one to hatch, announcing itself
on my fingertip, yellow mantle sliming my print,

minuscule eyes staring beyond me. Impossible
to know what cuttlefish see. Doppelgänger.

Pitching it as part of my musical score.
The algorithms of ocean currents differ

in their salinity and temperature.
You might want to acclimatise.

*

Each note is a rupture point.
Hearing of the 36cm eyeball they found,

it was the rest of the squid's body I imagined.
All these chain links couple our momentary collision.

I don't know how far the life-jacket
light has come, or who it went dark on;

how big once the kelp, or lump of seacoal
deafening in its break into two.

The sheet of metal I mistook for fish skin
hammered scales from the bauxite mines

still sharp against the dull call of desire.
I am listening too hard. All I hear is static

and what can I say to that?
Let me begin again.

Some days wind and tide spew shrapnel up the beach—on others these snappings of garish flakes hook

themselves to a retreating wave—drawn back under—away out of the bay on tides faster than a man can

[33]

Sea-drift

Yolk, blurry eye in its dull black tough-as-plastic
pouch. The egg sac is dented but not split.

Having alighted at my feet half in half out
of the grind of water, gas and mangled string,

it stares past me to the migrants who rode the easterlies
here and bore enough children to ensure five generations.

Washed by this wheezing ebb and flood I wonder how,
after all their efforts, I might consider being a full stop—

the size of one of the millions
of diatoms, bristle-strung in the water

producing a generation a day, absorbing sunlight,
emitting oxygen in an unfolding spiral of dot-to-dots

free from the tangle of fishing line I've pocketed
before springing from their clamouring advance.

run—bits of computer, biros, scraps of cars, satellite butts and buildings ride sand, waves, megaripples—

Spectral

Tens of millions of carbon-stitching
larvae and adult
plankton as indistinguishable
hunkered
inhaling as woman: exhaling as girl.

Looking as a four-year-old might
without the focus of glasses
at this waterbauble left behind
by sea backcombing saltmarsh,
I see pixels
multicoloured cells cohering
around this grassblade tip
refracting a limpet's trail
compassing home.

Mother and daughter of this place
ebb-dragged
and flood-ripped open,
my hands hammering and listening
will pull a fish from the washed-up yew
spines carved bark
scales chiselled
from having thrashed against tides
against all likelihood
to equip itself for flight and depth.

coils fuming—flexing nurdles—the bedrock of plastic manufacture—foam from drains and container ships

Towards a Stranding

I do not know myself as a mother, how different I could be: walking away rather than towards. It is too late to change my mind. Guttered by an ebb-tide leaching fertilisers infiltrating all bearings.

Whale plouters from one side of the bay to the other: an hour or breath away. Any one of us can lose navigational skills.

I used to relish thinking I might be infertile. Made avoiding motherhood an ethical act. Slipping across algae, I cannot judge the rise and fall of seabed: of ocean temperature, salinity.

Side on, white-flanked in diminishing light, in the wet-backed mud folding into creases: whale's muscular compass unfolding.

Flood pluming from river mouth to microscopic mouth into fasterthanafishcanswim mouth: particulates accumulate with every gulp — up to the lipids that should keep whale buoyant. Not bloating. Dissembling.

I do not want to get too close. I do not want to stop. I want to be enfolded by the night.

It's all very well saying that, but it's another thing when you're dying. The worst imaginings pleat into coastal sediment and open ocean from my landfill. There are always other stories to tell.

tough enough to reach the Irish Sea—looping polymers gleam chains of cosmetics and cleaning products

Stressed females breed earlier and later in life. The demise of one species makes space for another.

Grief is circular swimming. Whale without offspring is woman without. A crackle: oxygen expelling from mud: flesh whittled by currents to somehow endure. In the quiet rendition of water coiling, every movement appears to recede: every moment.

Pollutants lactate down the pod efficiently as carcasses upcycle as fodder. I seethe water. Closer, face furs. Methane. Salt. Drought. A sweetening of air too sweet, cloying and thick.

Muscled ground is undoing. Fish bones and sealscrag scour an approach: ghost shrimp. Whelk close. A call for the curtained ripples to sleep: closing vibrations bind tongues, the coupling channel.

We have few predators as persistent as the particulates which stockpile in tissue. There they disrupt ovaries, buck biomagnetism.

Feeling for where body fits and when it slides apart is a slow metabolism: a question of who possesses whom. There are always other stories to tell. Runnels of mud: gullies: arteries: everything comes alongside. And slows: withdrawing: arriving

—indistinguishable from bubbles of air or algae—spunk of gas, coal and oil—bristling tentacles of ancient

Holding (Fishing Baulk)

Whether I begin at the lighthouse or inland at Plover Hill,

or if the first hole was cast by hand between rocks,

once larger, less barnacled, more musseled,

in the middle of a slab of pink bedrock that erodes faster
out of the water than in (look to the keeper's cottage for proof),
I do not know.

I continue as a constellation of holes
shallow openings

pauses in the ground
interrupted by broken stakes

(the height of fossilised shins: of ankles: of lugworm debris)
uprights for willow fencing no longer held.

Each pause a different length, marking

a curve of receptacles
also filled with water: air: algae: grit: mud
when the tide's shrunk. How much a body can hold.

Today the invisible is in relief.

Ancient monument of a thousand holes:
memorial of absence: woven branches: fish
(I am the fish that got away): a singular pearly eel.

Absence is what makes me.

I hold the story, despite tide, passed between tides

between old man with walking stick (this place's son)
and newcomer woman in love with this stretch
that's a receptacle itself.
(I receive it and)

sunlight free from millennia of compression—in the warm northerly flow of the Gulf Stream breakdown

[38]

I keep alive
King John, the lepers, and monks proclaiming
impregnation a greater crime than murder.

I cross channels scrabbled out of rock piles

walled and gated to stop sluicing from the dug-out pond.
I hold the thrashing salmon, flounder and trapped plaice

no longer here.
I hold plankton in water-plugged hollows
that may still be here.

I am overlooked by men repairing the lighthouse, for whom a hole
is something to fill.

A delay of stakes
of broken wood, rotting with weed, some sawn short,
guy-roped to this greybrown baulk: closer to the moon

than tomorrow, I am the assumption
of tidal flow.

I withhold: take hold:

refuge: drilling half a kilometre: eight hundred years.

Weightless (of course)
yet weighted with all that came before. I am as water carries itself.

I know as water.

Silent as holes relaying the story.

is slow—even slower in the chill of the Norwegian Current—year on year—sluggish—Atlantic drifting

evaporating, condensing, precipitating—plastic's lifespan is as yet unknown—unfixed—as the Arctic—

Sea of whiteness, as glacier

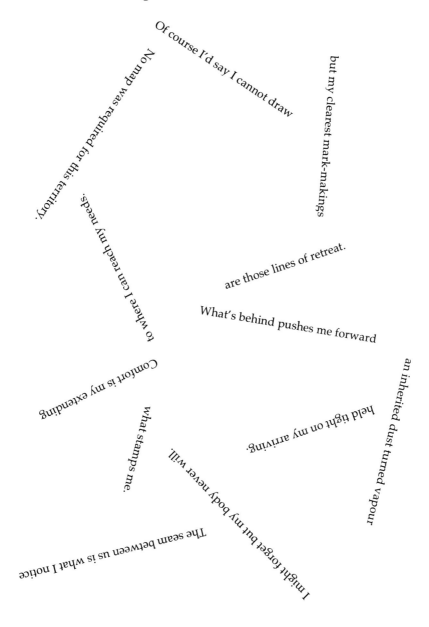

Of course I'd say I cannot draw

but my clearest mark-makings

No map was required for this territory.

to where I can reach my needs.

are those lines of retreat.

What's behind pushes me forward

an inherited dust turned vapour

Comfort is my extending

what stamps me.

held tight on my arriving.

I might forget but my body never will.

The seam between us is what I notice

a looping—gaseous exchange ocean—the most visible—countless streamings in global branching

[41]

melt
in which ice still holds the Arctic

This shallow ocean, stumped by hills eddying a heartbeat,
is where life rises.

                              One possible future: I look
into a berg: ice pixelated, grainy blue and grey.

There's me inside. Blue eyes swimming. Magnified.
I can't tell if I'll disappoint

anyone anything depending on me, or
                              me depending on me.

                  I'm not used to being lost.
Shoreline tells me the lie of the land.

Here I'll need my periphery to document what I can't read.
The more I think about words the more uneasy I feel.

I will use the ice as ink, to damp-shadow the page as
        squid fluoresce the cold.

—mini-revolutions—as overlooked as violated—this surging northwards—these bitty berg bombings—

Cloak

More gauze
than younger skin
harried salt-veined crystal
or ash, and yes, wrinkle-stitched by
ghostly

inex-
plicable cir-
cuitry. I will not be
unbuttoned, mined or sold. To be
ignored

does not
make mute. My brine
cannot fade nor tear, but
calcifies or dissolves those within.

of surface water that will become Arctic—of deeper water that will have been Arctic—frozen hinge—

It could be worse next year. It could be better.

I'd rather let stones tell the stories

of how learning to swim in water greasy with ice
can reach the same speed as walking across rubble.
                    Balance
as breath. Shallow if fast.

Hairline fractures, red
microscopic crucifixes vaulting the sea around me,
critter me, as I follow, nose to tail.

By the time I'm old
I'll know the tattoos under my skin: the collar
stitched tag: tracker magnets along the axis of head—trunk—flank.
Feel me.

My body releasing water
I stream water—becoming voltage

discovering how far to swim without knowing
what's at the close

of water that percolates the cracks in igneous rocks
and freezing, splits them into pages
thick grey folios opening.

Last winter adds its silk
to the record,
deposits a thinly crisping script.
The world is not dead yet.

icy water becoming heavier and downwelling—sinking as deep ocean currents, southwards slowing—

melt
in which the background is felt more than it's seen

Paper is a different kind of dissolving. The water in it
                     hooks the water in me

              rubbing away at my testimony
   to restore the pulped diction of wood.   Crumpling

  white space, its hours, brings distances closer.
          The weight of a ghost is tidal.

I ought to be indebted, but calving punches the waterline
          another line of defence lost.

Ripples become creases, wrinkles beyond
        the berg's interval.   Berg cavity

  is rung with sounds I don't understand.
Its light scatters as air bubbles, the tightest blue

bearing the exhalation of creatures I wouldn't recognise
who must have swum alongside the ice crystallising.

       A surge of oxygen baffles.   Burnt hydrogen
furs the back of my teeth. Magnetic makes me jittery.

I can feel methane grieving from my skin.
   Listen.   Harder.

The lines shadows cast are spiky and shortening. Stalactites
        I compass.   Ink. Gradient. Sun.

bright splinters above—dull particles below—this plasticity insures against decay and disease—

[45]

melt
in which things lie dormant

There's less room for me in the berg
turning jelly, turning walrus, turning plane, depending

where I stand. Squat.   Me swelling
as my surrounding hiss-drips in pinpricks. I buckle to fit.

Yes, I'm a forecast I don't want to admit.   How did it arrive?
  I compass.   Need to keep an eye on the time.

Ink. Gradient. Sun.   This cold body contains the fluid
                contains the currency containing me.

I've thrashed in seas, amniotic and oceanic
                          but now

what am I not doing that needs to be done?
How a thought wriggles, kicks. A missile multiplies.

Is it wrong to want it to happen far quicker than the drawn out
    ache below the surface?

not yet disappeared—yet not functioning as intended—the Arctic—hinge of what will become—

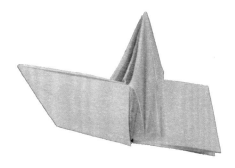

hinge of what will have been—circling plastics—some days wind and tide spew—others upwell—north—

Echolocation

We will plunge in one gulp
to where sound commutes us
on phonic lips.

Sea moves with many tongues.
Pressure loads.

For all the breath the sea gives me
when I'm out of it—for the temper
of ever-widening circles
like those we left on the surface
(each a death folded back into the body)
                —I do not belong.

The whale of my womb pulls me down
her orbit clobbers my throat.
She will reveal no one to distinguish jellies
from carrier bag, ooze from oil.
Filaments greentease from trench slits.
In this warp there's no identifying
a clutch of unfertilised eggs
we may not find in the sediment.

This isn't why I've come so far.

At my age I want
to discover the vacuum that prises
illimitable sense from economic sense—
that gulf between craving for transformation
and the rational reasons not to.

It will take a second, a third.
I am used to failure. We will dive again.

a walrus outlives the billiard ball—in the early twenty-first century—the viable is cheap and awayable—

melt
in which I explain my flight north

I followed the mackerel halibut cod swimming
seven kilometres a year further north.

How a thought wriggles. My hunger born of curiosity.
Access to money. I chose to travel to where the spinning slows.

        And below, my destination unscrolling
from the press of a forehead against aeroplane window

on a flight freighting me on the updraft of millennia,
        emitting a slew of carbon

equivalent to the annual output of a woman in India.
Thousands of litres of shoreline furrow from the engine's heat.

Oilman. Tourist. I take up space in a way I do not always feel.
        Blue eyes swimming.

molluscs hitch on torn sacking—plastics promising a cultural democracy—flowing polewards—pluming

[49]

melt
in which a fjord is not as expected

However much I shake my head
everything will become anothering and engraining.

Mud unshakeable. Water in mud hooks the water in me.
Today repeats a slither at a time. My forehead pressed. Rung

with sounds as the spinning slows.   I lose years
count back to innocence.   Nothing is innocent now.

Body a cavity   frost-torching my back.
Ocean tanks, nibbling my mud-smeared berg.

I ought to be travelling in the direction I face.
There's that flickering below the surface.

Rivers running faster than ever and I'm slurring mud
counting on a landfall that doesn't fit the shape in my head.

Wellingtons branded 'Aggressor' make me unsure
what shape I'll be in three hours from now.

I can't think fast enough.
Forests of polyps shunted on the tide, skeletal

coral the size of tiny fingers clutching
ninety million years rising out of the mud.

southwards—gyrating Atlantic loop—invisible as it swirls—attracting other persistent organic pollutants

Splint

Although it's difficult
to speak your language, I hear your call to arms and mouth
its music while its sense does not latch
yet. I do remember
how the cards, for you, presented a fish, for me, death. Your power
is a slender body of longing, unbidden, scaling
from the declared state of urgency that grafts us together
an ocean apart.

falling to the seafloor, leaking component chemicals back into dark watery mud—upwelling—to wreathe

[51]

Coccolithophore

Scraping my wet limbs
        grains of cathedrals
     that may never be built

This marine snow leaves the water with me
becoming winter to a distant seabed.
     Summer in another era.

There is no shame in a faith
         in what cannot be seen.

   Salt water, its stinging translucence
chisels my touch   sieving
              the ellipses

   —what is wonder if not unspoken—

of each algal pinhead
       thickening to the sea-change:
   acid as provocation to survival.

   A speed beyond sight
       and early days yet
  nevertheless I hope with the giant blue O
of an open mouthed planet.

miles out at sea—the discarded pulverised into microscopic debris by currents and waves—riding the

melt
in which comfort is sought

I find myself wanting
to hold (be held by) a body

                       as fleeting as mine
in the face of something too large to see.

The smallest algae will survive these conditions.
                    Their resistance to sinking.

So small I might not count.
Turn me   smaller than small.

Multitude defends.   Breathing is believing.
A comma of chlorophyll, many commas

punctuate many ripples amongst a legion
of crossing streams falling to sediment.

  Snow.   Millions coiling
across the glass parent that'll never be full.

Every exhale extends: nine months, a year, decades.
I find myself wanting to hold and be held.

Atlantic to populate uninhabited shores—so tiny targeting sieves remove similar-sized plankton

from the water—plankton that absorbs carbon dioxide—that produces our every second breath

melt
in which cold water downwells

Water as arteries, chaining into itself across bodies
within my body unfolding, making translating messy.

     I don't know which of me I am.   My best
     needs more time to incubate. Ice time. What time

as the water around me pools into the water with salt?
I hear it sinking. It'll not settle. All traces

     of me thinning.   I want to be counted. Rung
with the sounds of too many streams.

The ice in the water dilutes the salt.
And who knows what will be where then.

Jolting awake to the dark:
               :these shapes don't fit.

                  I slack jaw. I gawp
circling. Turn upside, smaller than small.

Ice eyes swimming. I upturn. Return. About
body be wilded.   Tend to this instant

of babble.   In its ink I taste
a weight of knots and holes older than speech.

There's no umbilical cord in the ocean. No anchor
chaining me to this or that.

—looping south as deep ocean currents—as saltier waters untouched by wind—surface microbeads

melt
in which I sediment

Loose bone. Smashed bone. Only the dead
are visible here.   It cannot be my desire

to shed the routine of sunrise sundown,
not wanting to keep an eye on time.

Like wanting to want no country to belong to.
The language of my soul is not that of my mind.

What to do with the gift of death
          its wave bearing down? Unasked for. Melt

or turn me: each doubt offers refuge.
                    I interference. I static.

I searching the bones of light.   Hear it circling,
the distance between one breath of absurdity

and a dive-long life-long descent
into the cartilage of my armour, splitting it

to ring in a child's voice, ice thin:
don't make me.

attached by static to microplants—eaten by crustaceans—eaten by squid—eaten by seal—eaten by

Mantle

Darkness to leach through layers of thermal fat and fleece muffling mobility, in a slowing down of body so deep it forces mind to unwind with it and open its creases—so dark those lost secrets can't distinguish between the night of hidden and of surface, and float, first as the scratch and itch of old wool, then as the brittle air slapped when the garment is abandoned and then,

well, I could guess—but I doubt I'd ever put it back on again. Everything would be different after that. Thin and loose, ready to slide off me. Rows of trees falling into sea, rock to shale, or buildings ready to crumble under heat or frost. I would marvel it had covered or insulated anything, adore it.

whale—or upcycling through salmon or turtles or shark or—or—ocean most visible—no plastic produced

Whitecap

a remembrance: skin slicked in bright currency   swept on
nothing to clutch.   In water seeming so very new.   Makes me so.
A dual impossibility.   A polishing of bearings   stripped vertical
easily spun.   Spills and leaks   sieved by distance   by coral   by
sponge   and feathers greased   far from any rupture.   This is
no pristine wash   but a remembrance of this floating   I became
so good at   flashes   almost stardust   aerosol up and   always
I am oily   with fluency   from one gulf to another   thousands
of miles   millions of gallons   decades   apart.   Memories
accumulate   become viscous.   This is a remembrance: stripped
harmless   seeking warmth.   Autumnal sea   willowed ripples
into rings of our years.   I comply   with a pressing persistence.

has disappeared—synthetic fibres washed out of clothes—into gyres miles out at sea—replicate

melt
in which the passage is uncharted

     I cannot stop. Nomadic eye   could be wrong
to trust ocean as motherboard, powering

   the swing to slime me from the colour of sky,
tumbling to mountains of bone, mud of sequestration.

Indebted. Charged, I   flickering   rolling
                   into distances impossible

to calculate. This water has no contours
in the dive-long, many lives-long age of mammals and

beyond to the boneless.   Galaxies of plankton.
Pinholes of light   lance me to smithereens.

     Uselessness turns me to anything.
Tomorrow I'll be born spooking.   A body of potential.

The water in spate breaks the water in me
          and water in ocean with all its little seas.

phytoplankton—become incidental fodder for zooplankton—disable motility, bloat stomachs, render

[59]

creatures sterile—at each transfer toxicity increases—upcycling to human—nothing is wasted—

pulled north—for polar waters to sink—enfolded in the efficient conveyor—one of many gyres—

[61]

indistinguishable from bubbles of air—upwelling south—pulled north—engulfed—what will become—

and how I will have found myself plankton, dividing between water and air

Elements